Title: The Ultimate Guide to Making Money Online: Strategies, Tips, and Techniques

I0845225

Richard L. McKenzie

Introduction

Welcome to the ultimate guide to making money online: strategies, tips, and techniques In today's digital age, the opportunities to earn a living from home are endless. Whether you are looking to supplement your income or replace your full-time job, this book is a comprehensive roadmap for navigating the vast and ever-evolving world of online entrepreneurship. From affiliate marketing and e-commerce to freelance work and digital products, it explores proven strategies, shares expert tips, and delves into the most effective techniques to help you achieve success in the lucrative online money-making realm. Get ready to unlock the potential of the Internet and discover the power of turning your passion and skills into a sustainable source of income. Embark on this exciting journey together and pave the way to financial freedom in the digital world. Whether it's to supplement your income or build a full-time online business, the possibilities for making money online are virtually endless. But navigating the world of online income generation can be overwhelming and confusing. That's where this ultimate guide comes in.

Chapter 1: Introduction to Making Money Online

This chapter explores the great potential of making money online, the various ways to generate income on the Internet, and the benefits and challenges of making money online. Understanding the online income landscape is the first step in building a successful online business.

Possibilities of Making Money Online

1. Freelancing: Platforms such as Upwork, Fiverr, and Freelancer connect freelancers with clients looking for writing, graphic design, programming, marketing, and other services.
2. Online surveys and reviews: participating in online surveys, product reviews, and website testing can be a way to earn a small amount of money or gift cards.

3. Content creation: if you enjoy creating content, you can start a blog, YouTube channel, or podcast. Monetization options include advertising, sponsorship, affiliate marketing, and viewer donations.

4. Affiliate marketing: advertise other companies' products and receive a commission for each sale made through your affiliate link. Many companies offer affiliate programs.

5. Online courses and e-books: if you have expertise in an area, you can create and sell online courses and e-books through platforms such as Udemy, Teachable, and Amazon Kindle Direct Publishing.

6. E-commerce and dropshipping: set up an online store and sell physical or digital goods. Dropshipping allows you to sell goods without stock; instead, goods are shipped directly from the supplier to the customer.

7. Stock photos: if you are a photographer, you can sell your photos on stock photo sites such as Shutterstock or Adobe Stock.

8. Remote work: many traditional jobs can now be done remotely: job sites such as Remote OK and We Work Remotely offer remote work opportunities.

9. Virtual assistance: as virtual assistants, they provide administrative support services to businesses and entrepreneurs.

10. Social media management: maintaining social media accounts for businesses and individuals. Many organizations are willing to pay for help with their online presence.

11. Cryptocurrency and trading: although risky, some people make money trading, investing, and mining cryptocurrency.

12. Gaming and streaming: if you enjoy video games, you can earn income through advertising, subscriptions, and viewer donations on platforms such as Twitch and YouTube Gaming.

13. While there are plenty of legitimate opportunities, it's important to note that there are also scammers out there. Be vigilant and do thorough research before investing time and money in online opportunities. Additionally, success often takes time, effort, and a consistent commitment to building your online presence and business.

Different ways to earn income online

There are many ways to earn an income online, and the opportunities continue to evolve as technology advances. Here are some of the most common ways. Keep in mind that the internet environment is dynamic, and new opportunities may arise later on. Here is a list of the various ways to earn income online:

→ Freelancing:
→ Platforms like Upwork, Freelancer, and Fiverr allow individuals to offer their skills and services to people around the world.
→ Online marketplaces: Marketplaces on the internet where people can sell their products and services to others:
→ Platforms such as Etsy (handmade goods), eBay (miscellaneous goods), and Amazon (retail goods) allow people to sell their products.

→ Blogs:
→ Monetizing a blog through advertising, sponsored content, affiliate marketing, and selling digital products

→ Affiliate marketing:
→ Promoting other people's products and earning a commission for every sale or lead generated by your referral

→ YouTube channel:
→ Creating videos on YouTube and monetizing them through advertising, sponsorship, and product sales.

→ Podcasting:
→ Generate revenue through sponsorship, listener donations, and premium content subscriptions.

→ Online courses:

➔ Create and sell courses on platforms like Udemy, Teachable, and Skillshare.

➔ E-books and self-publishing:
➔ Write and sell e-books on platforms like Amazon Kindle or self-publish through websites.

➔ Stock photography:
➔ Sell high-quality photos on stock photography sites like Shutterstock and Adobe Stock.

➔ Dropshipping:
➔ Run an online store without having to carry stock by partnering with a fulfillment supplier.

➔ Cryptocurrency trading:
➔ Buying and selling cryptocurrencies on various exchanges.

➔ Telecommuting:
➔ Working remotely for a company and providing services such as virtual assistance, customer support, and programming.

➔ Social media management:
➔ Managing company and personal social media accounts.

➔ Web design and development:
➔ Providing web design and development services to clients.

➔ Virtual assistance:
➔ Providing remote administrative support to businesses and entrepreneurs.

➔ Online surveys and reviews:
➔ Taking paid online surveys or writing reviews about products and services.

➔ Gig economy applications:

➔ Join gig economy platforms like Uber, Lyft, and TaskRabbit for flexible, on-demand jobs.

➔ Remote consulting:

➔ Provide expertise in a specific field through online consulting services.

➔ Membership websites:

➔ Start a membership website or community and provide exclusive content to members.

➔ Real estate crowdfunding:

➔ Invest in real estate projects through online crowdfunding platforms.

➔ Before adopting any approach, it is crucial to research and understand the requirements, potential revenue, and risks associated with each opportunity. In addition, the internet landscape is constantly changing, so staying informed about emerging trends is essential for long-term success.

Advantages and challenges of making money online

Making money online has its own unique advantages and challenges. Here is a breakdown of some of the key considerations:

- **Advantages**
- Flexibility:
- Online businesses often offer flexibility in terms of working hours and locations. Many online jobs and businesses allow you to work from anywhere with an internet connection.

- Global reach:

- The internet provides access to a global audience. This greatly expands the market for your products, services, and skills and allows you to reach customers and clients worldwide.

- Low overhead costs:
- Many online ventures have lower start-up costs than traditional brick and mortar businesses. In some cases, a physical storefront may not needed, and costs related to inventory, utilities, and other overhead expenses can be reduced.

- Diverse revenue streams:
- Online platforms offer a variety of ways to monetize skills, content, and products. Diversifying revenue streams can provide stability and reduce reliance on a single source of income.

- Automation and scalability:
- Automation tools and digital platforms allow businesses to scale efficiently. Once established, some online businesses can operate with less manual labor.

- Access to information and resources:
- The internet provides a wealth of information and resources, making it easier for individuals to learn new skills, learn about market trends, and access tools to enhance their online presence.

Challenges

Competition
The online space is often highly competitive. Standing out from the crowd of competitors requires strategic planning, a unique value proposition, and effective marketing.

1. Concerns about security and privacy:
   Online transactions and activities involve security and privacy risks. Individuals and businesses need to take steps to protect sensitive information and ensure a secure online presence.

2. Changing algorithms and policies:
   Platforms and algorithms can change, affecting the visibility and access of online content. In addition, policies and regulations may affect certain online activities, and individuals will need to adapt their strategies.

3. Technical challenges:
Online ventures may face technical challenges, such as website outages, cybersecurity threats, and difficulties adapting to new technologies. Technical skills and support may be needed to overcome these issues.
Income insecurity:
Some online income streams, such as freelancing and affiliate marketing, are not stable. Income can be up and down, and it can take time to build a stable income stream.

4. Dependency on external platforms:
Depending on third-party platforms, such as social media and online marketplaces, for income can be risky. Changes in the policies and algorithms of these platforms can affect visibility and revenues.
Isolation and burnout:
Working online, especially alone, can lead to isolation. The flexibility of remote work also blurs boundaries and can lead to burnout if not managed effectively.

5. Scams and frauds:
The online world is not immune to scams and frauds. You need to be careful not to fall victim to a scam or phishing scam.
Success in making money online often requires a combination of skill, adaptability, and flexibility. Recognizing both the benefits and challenges will help you use the internet more effectively.

Chapter 2: Setting the Foundation

This section discusses the key elements that form the foundations of our journey. Whether it is a personal project, a business endeavor or a creative endeavor, it is important to lay a solid foundation for long-term success. This section will guide you through the key considerations and actions that will shape the course of your venture.

1. Clarify your purpose
Before you create something meaningful, it is crucial to clearly define your purpose. What is the driving force behind your project or goal? Understanding your purpose not only gives direction, but is also a constant source of motivation.

2. Set goals and objectives:
It is essential to set specific, measurable, achievable, relevant and time-bound (SMART) goals. These goals serve as milestones and help to monitor progress. Breaking large goals into smaller, more manageable tasks allows for a more organized approach.

3. Understand your audience:
Whether you are creating content, launching a product or pursuing a cause, it is important to know your audience. Identify your audience and understand their needs, preferences and pain points. Tailor your approach to resonate with your audience.

4. Market research:
Conduct thorough market research to gain insight into industry trends, competitors and potential business opportunities. This information is invaluable for making informed decisions and adapting to a dynamic environment.

5. Legal and regulatory considerations:
Familiarize yourself with the legal and regulatory aspects relevant to your venture. This includes business registration, intellectual property considerations, and compliance with local laws. If these issues are not addressed at an early stage, they can become complicated later.

6. Resource assessment:
Assess the resources required for the project, including financial, human, and technical resources. Assessing available resources and identifying potential gaps will enable you to plan effectively and avoid unforeseen problems.

7. Build a strong team:
If your startup involves collaboration, it is crucial that you have the right team. Look for people who can complement your skills and share your vision. Effective communication and a cohesive team are essential for success.

8. Financial planning:
Make a realistic budget that takes into account all expenses related to your startup. Consider potential sources of income and develop a financial plan in line with your goals. Monitor it regularly, and adjust your financial strategy as needed.

9. Technology and tools:
Depending on the project, identify the technology and tools required for implementation. Keep up to date with relevant developments to ensure the project remains competitive and efficient.

10. Risk analysis and mitigation:
Anticipate risks and challenges that may arise during the initiative.
Developing contingency plans to mitigate these risks will help you navigate
uncertainty with greater resilience.
By addressing these key elements, you can lay the foundations for a more
sustainable and successful venture. The following sections will explore
each element in more detail and provide practical insights and actionable
steps to guide you on your journey. Remember, a strong foundation sets
the stage for growth and innovation.

Identifying your skills, interests, and expertise.

- Step-by-step guide:
- Self-assessment Skills
- Analytical skills: Are you good at analyzing data, identifying trends, and making decisions based on data?

- Creativity: Can you come up with innovative and engaging content and advertising ideas?

- Technical skills: are you familiar with digital marketing tools, SEO, social media platforms, and other online marketing technologies?

- Communication skills: can you effectively communicate your ideas in writing, design, and verbally?

- Define Define your areas of interest:
- Content creation: do you like writing blog posts, creating videos, graphic design?

- Social media: Are you passionate about engaging with your audience on platforms like Facebook, Instagram, and Twitter?
- SEO (search engine optimization): Are you interested in optimizing your content for search engines and increasing visibility?

- Paid advertising: Are you interested in creating and managing online advertising campaigns?

- Education and training: Consider taking courses or gaining qualifications in specific areas of online marketing.

- Practical experience: gain practical experience through personal projects and working with others.

- Networking: connect with professionals in the field through social media, forums, and networking events.

- Stay up-to-date:
- The online marketing field is dynamic. Stay informed about industry trends, algorithm changes and new tools.

- Develop your expertise.
- Identify your niche: there are many different areas of online marketing. You can specialize in content marketing, social media management, email marketing or any other specific area.

- Personal branding: Build a personal brand within your chosen niche. Always deliver quality work and showcase your expertise.

- Evaluate results:
- Monitor success: track the results of your marketing activities. Use analytical tools to measure the effectiveness of your strategies.
- Adapt and improve: learn from both successes and failures. Think about what works best for your target audience and adjust your approach.

- Remember that online marketing is a broad field, and you can explore different directions before you find your niche. Continuous learning and adapting to evolving conditions are the keys to success in this dynamic industry.

Researching and analyzing online market trends

Researching and analyzing online market trends is crucial for staying competitive and making informed business decisions. Here's a guide on how to effectively conduct research and analysis:

Define Your Objectives:
- Clearly outline the goals of your research. Are you looking to identify emerging trends, understand customer behavior, or assess the competitive landscape?

Identify Key Metrics:
- Determine the key performance indicators (KPIs) relevant to your objectives. These might include website traffic, social media engagement, conversion rates, or industry-specific metrics.

Use Analytics Tools:
- Leverage analytics tools like Google Analytics, Adobe Analytics, or social media insights platforms to gather quantitative data on user behavior, website performance, and social media engagement.

Customer Surveys and Feedback:
- Collect qualitative data by conducting customer surveys or gathering feedback through customer support channels. Understanding customer needs and preferences is essential for identifying trends.

Competitor Analysis:
- Monitor your competitors' online activities. Analyze their digital marketing strategies, social media presence, content marketing efforts, and product/service offerings. Tools like SEMrush or Ahrefs can assist in competitor analysis.

Industry Reports and Publications:
- Stay informed about your industry by reading reports and publications from reputable sources. Industry reports often provide insights into market trends, challenges, and opportunities.

Social Media Listening:
- Use social media listening tools to track mentions of your brand, products, or industry-related keywords. This can help you understand what people are saying about your business and industry trends.

Google Trends:
- Explore Google Trends to identify search interest patterns over time. This tool can provide insights into the popularity of specific keywords and topics.

Stay Updated with News and Blogs:
- Regularly read industry news, blogs, and forums to stay up-to-date with the latest developments. Engaging with industry communities can also provide valuable insights.

Data Visualization:
- Use data visualization tools to present your findings in a clear and visually appealing manner. Charts, graphs, and infographics can make complex data more accessible.

Collaborate with Team Members:
- Foster collaboration within your team or organization. Different perspectives can lead to a more comprehensive understanding of market trends.

Regularly Review and Update:
- Market trends can change rapidly. Regularly review and update your research to ensure that your insights remain current and relevant.

By following these steps and continuously refining your approach, you can develop a robust system for researching and analyzing online market trends. This information is valuable for making informed business decisions and staying ahead in a dynamic digital landscape.

Understanding the legal and financial aspects of online income

Understanding the legal and financial aspects of online income is crucial for individuals and businesses engaged in various online activities. Here's a guide to help you navigate these aspects:

Legal Aspects:

Tax Obligations:
- Understand your tax obligations based on the country or region you operate in. Different jurisdictions may have varying tax laws regarding online income, including income tax, sales tax, and VAT.

Business Structure:
- Determine the appropriate legal structure for your online activities. This might include operating as a sole proprietorship, LLC, corporation, or other legal entities. Each structure has different legal implications and tax considerations.

Intellectual Property:
- Protect your intellectual property, such as trademarks, copyrights, and patents, especially if you are creating and selling digital products or services online.

Contracts and Agreements:
- Use clear and comprehensive contracts for any business transactions. Clearly outline terms of service, payment terms, delivery expectations, and any other relevant details.

Compliance with Regulations:
- Stay informed about industry-specific regulations and compliance requirements. This includes data protection laws,

online advertising regulations, and other relevant rules that may impact your online activities.

Online Privacy and Data Protection:

- Ensure compliance with data protection laws, especially if you collect and handle personal information. Implement privacy policies and secure data handling practices.

Digital Marketing Compliance:

- Adhere to regulations related to online advertising and marketing. This includes rules about disclosure, user consent, and fair advertising practices.

Customer Dispute Resolution:

- Have a clear process for handling customer disputes. This could involve setting up a customer support system and understanding chargeback procedures if applicable.

Financial Aspects:

Bookkeeping and Accounting:

- Keep accurate and up-to-date financial records. Use accounting software to track income, expenses, and taxes. This will facilitate easier financial management and tax reporting.

Budgeting:

- Develop a budget to manage your expenses effectively. Consider both fixed and variable costs associated with your online activities.

Payment Processing:

- Choose secure and reliable payment processors for handling online transactions. Understand the fees associated with each method and any currency conversion costs.

Emergency Fund:

- Establish an emergency fund for unexpected expenses or fluctuations in income. This provides a financial buffer during lean periods.

Investment and Retirement Planning:

- Consider investment options and retirement planning. This is important for individuals who generate online income as freelancers or entrepreneurs without traditional employer-sponsored retirement plans.

Insurance:

- Explore insurance options to protect your business and personal assets. This might include liability insurance, business insurance, or other coverage depending on your activities.

Local and International Tax Considerations:

- Understand the tax implications of earning income both locally and internationally. Consider consulting with a tax professional to ensure compliance with tax laws in different jurisdictions.

Record Keeping:

- Maintain organized financial records for auditing purposes and to provide a clear picture of your financial health.

By addressing these legal and financial aspects, you can create a solid foundation for your online income activities. It's advisable to seek professional advice, such as consulting with a tax accountant or legal expert, to ensure compliance with specific regulations and laws relevant to your situation

Chapter 3: Freelancing and Consulting

Leveraging your skills and expertise to offer services online can be a rewarding venture. Whether you are a freelancer, consultant, coach, or service provider, here are steps you can take to establish and market your online services:

Identify Your Skills and Expertise:
- Clearly define the skills and expertise you want to leverage. This could include writing, graphic design, programming, consulting, coaching, marketing, and more.

Build an Online Presence:
- Create a professional online presence. Develop a website that showcases your skills, experience, and the services you offer. Ensure that your website is user-friendly and mobile-responsive.

Create a Portfolio:
- Showcase your work in a portfolio. Include examples of projects, case studies, or testimonials that demonstrate your skills and expertise. This provides potential clients with a tangible understanding of what you can offer.

Define Your Services:
- Clearly define the services you are offering. Develop packages or service tiers if applicable, and provide transparent pricing information. Make it easy for potential clients to understand what you provide.

Set Up Online Platforms:
- Utilize online platforms and marketplaces that align with your services. This might include freelancing platforms like Upwork, Fiverr, or specialized platforms in your industry.

Networking:
- Network with other professionals in your industry. Join relevant online communities, forums, and social media groups. Engage

in conversations, share your expertise, and connect with potential clients or collaborators.

Content Marketing:
- Share valuable content related to your expertise. Start a blog, create informative videos, or host webinars. This not only establishes you as an authority in your field but also attracts potential clients.

Social Media Marketing:
- Leverage social media platforms to promote your services. Share your work, engage with your audience, and use targeted advertising to reach potential clients.

Optimize for Search Engines (SEO):
- Ensure that your website and online profiles are optimized for search engines. This can help potential clients find you when searching for services in your niche.

Offer Free Resources:
- Provide free resources or introductory services to attract clients. This could be a free consultation, a downloadable guide, or a trial version of your service.

Client Testimonials:
- Request and showcase client testimonials. Positive feedback from previous clients builds trust and credibility with potential clients.

Online Payment Systems:
- Set up secure and convenient online payment systems. This makes it easy for clients to pay for your services and ensures a smooth transaction process.

Continuous Learning:
- Stay updated with industry trends and advancements. Continuous learning and improvement keep your skills relevant and enhance the value you can offer to clients.

Professionalism and Communication:
- Maintain professionalism in all communications. Respond promptly to inquiries, set clear expectations, and communicate effectively with clients.

Legal Considerations:
- Ensure that you have clear contracts and agreements in place for your services. Address payment terms, deliverables, and any other relevant details. Consult with legal professionals if needed.

Remember, building a successful online service business takes time and persistence. Consistently delivering high-quality work and providing excellent customer service are key factors in building a positive reputation and attracting clients.

Finding clients and projects through freelancing platforms

Freelancing platforms can be a great way to find clients and projects, offering a streamlined way for freelancers to connect with those seeking their skills. Here's a step-by-step guide on how to effectively find clients and projects through freelancing platforms:

1. Create a Strong Profile:

- Professional Photo and Bio: Use a high-quality, professional photo and write a compelling bio that highlights your skills, experience, and what makes you unique.
- Portfolio Showcase: Upload examples of your best work to showcase your skills. Include diverse samples to demonstrate your range.
- Skills and Expertise: Clearly list your skills and expertise. Use keywords relevant to your niche to make your profile easily discoverable.

2. Optimize for Search:

- Use Relevant Keywords: Incorporate keywords that potential clients might use to search for services like yours. This can enhance your visibility in search results.
- Specialize if Possible: If you have a niche or specialization, highlight it in your profile. Many clients are looking for specialists.

3. Set Up Job Alerts:

- Define Your Criteria: Use the platform's job alert feature to receive notifications about projects that match your skills and preferences. Customize your alert settings to ensure you receive relevant opportunities.

4. Craft Winning Proposals:

- Personalization: Tailor your proposals to each client's specific needs. Avoid generic responses and show that you've read and understood the project requirements.
- Highlight Relevant Experience: Emphasize your relevant experience and provide examples of similar projects you've successfully completed.
- Clear Pricing: Clearly outline your pricing structure. If possible, break down the costs for different components of the project.
- Ask Questions: Demonstrate your interest in the project by asking thoughtful questions. This not only shows engagement but also helps you better understand the client's needs.

5. Build a Solid Reputation:

- Deliver High-Quality Work: Consistently provide high-quality work to build positive reviews and ratings. Positive feedback is crucial for attracting new clients.
- Meet Deadlines: Adhere to project timelines. Meeting or exceeding deadlines enhances your reliability.

6. Engage in the Community:

- Participate in Forums and Discussions: Many freelancing platforms have forums or community sections. Engage in discussions, share your expertise, and offer help to others. This can increase your visibility.
- Networking: Connect with other freelancers and clients on the platform. Networking can lead to referrals and collaborations.

7. Offer Additional Services:

- Upsell Your Services: If appropriate, offer additional services beyond the initial project. This can lead to long-term client relationships.

8. Stay Professional:

- Clear Communication: Maintain clear and prompt communication with clients. Address any concerns or questions they may have.
- Professionalism: Be professional in all interactions. A positive and professional demeanor contributes to a good working relationship.

9. Request Feedback:

- Ask Satisfied Clients for Reviews: Once you've successfully completed a project, politely ask clients for feedback and reviews. Positive reviews build trust with future clients.

10. Continuous Improvement:

- Learn and Adapt: Stay updated on industry trends and continually improve your skills. This positions you as a reliable and knowledgeable freelancer.

By following these steps, you can enhance your visibility, attract clients, and secure projects on freelancing platforms. Remember that building a strong reputation takes time, so be patient and persistent in your efforts.

Building a successful freelance business and expanding your client base

Building a successful freelance business and expanding your client base involves a combination of skills, strategies, and ongoing efforts. Here are some tips to help you grow your freelance business:

Define Your Niche:
- Identify your specific skills and strengths.
- Focus on a niche where you can provide exceptional value.

Build an Impressive Portfolio:
- Showcase your best work in an online portfolio.
- Highlight projects relevant to your target clients.

Create a Professional Online Presence:
- Develop a professional website.
- Optimize your LinkedIn profile and other relevant social media.

Networking:
- Attend industry events, both online and offline.
- Join relevant forums and groups to connect with potential clients and other freelancers.

Utilize Freelance Platforms:
- Create profiles on popular freelance platforms like Upwork, Freelancer, or Fiverr.
- Complete your profile with a professional photo, detailed description, and a list of your skills.

Offer Exceptional Service:
- Provide high-quality work to your clients.
- Encourage satisfied clients to leave reviews and testimonials.

Effective Communication:
- Respond promptly to client inquiries.
- Clearly communicate project details, timelines, and expectations.

Set Clear Terms and Conditions:
- Clearly define your rates, payment terms, and project scope.
- Use contracts to formalize agreements and protect both parties.

Upsell and Cross-Sell:
- Offer additional services to existing clients.
- Cross-sell related services that complement your primary offerings.

Invest in Self-Promotion:
- Use content marketing to showcase your expertise.
- Create informative blog posts, videos, or social media content.

Continuous Learning:
- Stay updated on industry trends and new skills.
- Attend workshops, webinars, and courses to enhance your expertise.

Collaborate with Other Freelancers:
- Partner with freelancers in complementary fields.
- They can refer clients to you, and vice versa.

Ask for Referrals:
- Request referrals from satisfied clients.
- Consider offering incentives for successful referrals.

Optimize for Search Engines:
- Ensure your website and profiles are optimized for relevant keywords.
- This can improve your visibility on search engines.

Diversify Your Income Streams:
- Consider offering a mix of services or products.
- This can help stabilize your income during slow periods.

Attend Local Events:
- Attend local meetups, conferences, or networking events.
- Connect with potential clients in your area.

Stay Consistent:

- **Consistency is key to building a successful freelance business.**
- **Regularly update your portfolio, social media, and other online profiles.**

Remember, building a successful freelance business takes time and effort. It's essential to continually assess and refine your strategies based on your experiences and the evolving needs of your target market.

Chapter 4: Creating and Selling Digital Products

Developing digital products such as e-books, online courses, and software

Developing digital products like e-books, online courses, and software involves a strategic and systematic approach. Here's a general guide for each type of product:

1. E-books:

a. **Identify Your Niche:**

- Understand your target audience.
- Identify a specific problem or need your e-book will address.

b. **Content Creation:**

- Plan the structure of your e-book.
- Create high-quality, valuable content.
- Consider multimedia elements (images, charts, etc.).

c. **Design:**

- Invest in professional design or use tools like Canva.
- Ensure compatibility with various devices and e-book readers.

d. **Distribution:**

- Choose a platform for distribution (Amazon Kindle, Apple Books, etc.).
- Consider creating a website for direct sales.

e. **Marketing:**

- Develop a marketing strategy to promote your e-book.
- Leverage social media, email marketing, and collaborations.

2. Online Courses:

a. Define Your Course:

- Clearly define the learning objectives.
- Break content into manageable modules.

b. Create Content:

- Develop multimedia content (videos, presentations, quizzes).
- Consider interactivity for engagement.

c. Platform Selection:

- Choose a reliable online course platform (Udemy, Teachable, etc.).
- Ensure user-friendly navigation and compatibility.

d. Payment and Access:

- Set a pricing strategy.
- Implement secure payment gateways.
- Provide clear access instructions.

e. Engagement and Support:

- Incorporate discussion forums or Q&A sections.
- Offer customer support for technical issues.

f. Marketing:

- Use social media and content marketing to attract learners.
- Offer free previews or trials to encourage enrollment.

3. Software:

a. Idea and Planning:

- Clearly define the problem your software solves.
- Create a detailed plan including features and functionalities.

b. **Development:**

- Choose a suitable programming language and framework.
- Follow best coding practices.
- Consider agile development for flexibility.

c. **Testing:**

- Conduct thorough testing to ensure functionality and security.
- Gather user feedback for improvements.

d. **Deployment:**

- Choose a reliable hosting or deployment strategy.
- Ensure scalability for future growth.

e. **Marketing:**

- Develop a website or landing page for the software.
- Utilize digital marketing channels for promotion.
- Consider offering a freemium model or trial version.

f. **Support and Updates:**

- Provide customer support channels.
- Regularly update the software to fix bugs and add features.

General Tips:

- Legalities:
    - Ensure compliance with copyright and intellectual property laws.
    - Clearly outline terms of use.
- Feedback Loop:
    - Continuously gather feedback and iterate on your products.
    - Stay responsive to user needs and industry trends.
- Monetization:
    - Explore various monetization models (one-time purchase, subscription, freemium).

- Adjust pricing based on market feedback and competition.

Remember, the success of your digital products relies not only on their development but also on effective marketing, user engagement, and ongoing support.

Setting up an online store or e-commerce platform to sell digital products

Setting up an online store or e-commerce platform to sell digital products involves several key steps. Here's a guide to help you get started:

1. Define Your Product and Target Audience:

- Clearly define the digital products you want to sell.
- Identify your target audience and understand their needs.

2. Choose a Platform:

- Select an e-commerce platform that supports digital product sales. Popular options include Shopify, WooCommerce (for WordPress), BigCommerce, and Gumroad.

3. Domain and Hosting:

- Choose a domain name that reflects your brand.
- Set up reliable hosting for your website.

4. Create Your Online Store:

- Customize the look and feel of your store. Most platforms provide themes you can modify.
- Set up product categories and organize your digital products.

5. Payment Gateways:

- Integrate a secure payment gateway to accept payments. Popular options include PayPal, Stripe, and Square.
- Ensure your platform supports digital product delivery upon successful payment.

6. Digital Product Delivery:

- Decide how you will deliver digital products. This could be through direct download links, email delivery, or a secure member area on your website.

7. Pricing and Promotions:

- Set competitive and reasonable prices for your digital products.
- Consider offering promotions or discounts to attract customers.

8. Security:

- Implement security measures to protect customer data and transactions.
- Use SSL certificates for secure connections.

9. Legal Considerations:

- Clearly outline your terms of service, refund policy, and privacy policy.
- Ensure compliance with relevant laws, especially regarding digital product sales.

10. Marketing:

- Develop a marketing strategy to drive traffic to your store. This can include social media, content marketing, email marketing, and search engine optimization (SEO).

11. Analytics:

- Set up analytics tools to track your website's performance and customer behavior. Google Analytics is a popular choice.

12. Customer Support:

- Provide clear and accessible customer support. This may include FAQs, live chat, or email support.

13. Regular Updates:

- Keep your website and product information up-to-date.
- Listen to customer feedback and make improvements accordingly.

14. Scaling:

- Plan for scalability as your business grows. Ensure your chosen platform can handle increased traffic and transactions.

15. Compliance:

- Ensure your store complies with industry regulations, such as GDPR for handling customer data.

16. Testing:

- Test your website thoroughly before launch to identify and fix any issues.

Remember to adapt these steps to the specific features and requirements of the e-commerce platform you choose. Regularly assess and optimize your store based on customer feedback and market trends.

Marketing and promoting digital products to reach a wider audience

Marketing and promoting digital products effectively involves a combination of strategic planning, targeted execution, and ongoing optimization. Here are some key strategies to help you reach a wider audience:

Understand Your Target Audience:
- Define your target audience clearly. Understand their needs, preferences, and behaviors.
- Create buyer personas to represent different segments of your audience.

Optimize Your Website and Landing Pages:
- Ensure your website is user-friendly, mobile-responsive, and optimized for search engines (SEO).
- Create compelling landing pages that clearly communicate the value proposition of your digital product.

Content Marketing:
- Develop high-quality, valuable content related to your digital product.
- Use a variety of content types, such as blog posts, videos, infographics, and podcasts.
- Share your content on your website, social media, and relevant online communities.

Social Media Marketing:
- Identify the social media platforms your target audience frequents.
- Create engaging and shareable content tailored to each platform.
- Use paid advertising on platforms like Facebook, Instagram, Twitter, or LinkedIn to reach a broader audience.

Email Marketing:
- Build and segment an email list.
- Send targeted and personalized email campaigns to promote your digital product.
- Use email automation to nurture leads and maintain engagement.

Influencer Marketing:
- Identify influencers in your industry or niche.
- Collaborate with influencers to promote your digital product.
- Influencers can help you reach a wider audience and build credibility.

Search Engine Marketing (SEM):
- Use paid advertising through platforms like Google Ads.
- Target keywords related to your digital product to appear in search results.
- Optimize your ad copy and landing pages for better conversion rates.

Affiliate Marketing:
- Set up an affiliate program to encourage others to promote your product.
- Offer commissions or incentives for successful referrals.

Customer Reviews and Testimonials:
- Encourage satisfied customers to leave reviews and testimonials.
- Display positive reviews on your website and marketing materials to build trust.

Webinars and Online Events:
- Host webinars or online events to showcase your digital product.
- Use these events to engage with your audience and address their questions.

Community Building:
- Create and participate in online communities related to your niche.
- Engage with your audience, answer questions, and share your expertise.

Analytics and Optimization:
- Use analytics tools to track the performance of your marketing efforts.
- Analyze data to identify what strategies are working and optimize your approach accordingly.

Remember to continuously adapt your strategies based on feedback and data analysis. The digital landscape is dynamic, so staying flexible and responsive is crucial for ongoing success.

Chapter 5: Affiliate Marketing

Understanding the concept of affiliate marketing and how it works

Affiliate marketing is a performance-based marketing strategy where businesses reward affiliates (partners or publishers) for driving traffic or sales to the business's products or services through the affiliate's marketing efforts. It's a mutually beneficial arrangement where both parties can earn money: the business gets more customers or sales, and the affiliate earns a commission for their efforts.

Here's a breakdown of how affiliate marketing works:

Parties Involved:
- **Merchant (Advertiser): This is the business or company that owns the product or service. The merchant decides to use affiliate marketing to promote its products and services.**
- **Affiliate (Publisher): This is the individual or company that promotes the merchant's products or services through various marketing channels.**

Joining an Affiliate Program:
- **The merchant sets up an affiliate program, providing a unique tracking ID or affiliate link for each affiliate.**
- **Affiliates join the program and receive their unique affiliate links, which track the traffic and sales they generate.**

Promotion by Affiliates:
- **Affiliates use various marketing channels to promote the merchant's products or services. This can include websites, blogs, social media, email marketing, and more.**
- **The affiliate incorporates their unique affiliate link in their promotional content.**

Tracking and Analytics:

- The affiliate link contains a unique identifier that allows the merchant to track the traffic and sales generated by each affiliate.
- Modern affiliate programs often use cookies or other tracking mechanisms to identify and credit the affiliate for referred customers.

Customer Clicks and Purchases:
- When a customer clicks on the affiliate's link and makes a purchase or performs a desired action (like signing up for a trial), the affiliate is credited for that sale or lead.

Commission Payment:
- The merchant pays the affiliate a commission for each sale or action generated through the affiliate's efforts.
- Commissions can be a percentage of the sale or a fixed amount per action, depending on the affiliate program.

Payment Models:
- There are various payment models in affiliate marketing, including:
    - Pay-Per-Sale (PPS): Affiliates earn a commission when the referred customer makes a purchase.
    - Pay-Per-Click (PPC): Affiliates earn a commission based on the number of clicks generated, regardless of whether a sale occurs.
    - Pay-Per-Lead (PPL): Affiliates earn a commission for generating leads, such as sign-ups or form submissions.

Affiliate marketing is a scalable and cost-effective way for businesses to expand their reach and increase sales, while affiliates have the opportunity to earn income without the need to create and maintain their own products. It's a popular and widely used strategy in the online business world.

Finding and joining affiliate programs in your niche

Finding and joining affiliate programs in your niche involves a few steps. Whether you have a blog, website, social media presence, or another platform, here's a general guide to help you identify and participate in affiliate programs:

Identify Your Niche:
- Clearly define your niche or the topic of your content. This could be anything from health and wellness to technology or fashion.

Research Affiliate Programs:
- Use search engines to look for affiliate programs in your niche. You can search for "[Your Niche] affiliate programs" or "[Product/Service] affiliate program."
- Consider using affiliate program directories and networks that compile various programs. Examples include:
  - ClickBank
  - CJ Affiliate (formerly Commission Junction)
  - ShareASale
  - Rakuten Marketing

Check Companies You Already Use:
- If you already use products or services related to your niche, check if those companies offer affiliate programs. Many companies have affiliate programs, even if they are not widely advertised.

Explore Niche-Specific Affiliate Networks:
- Some industries have specialized affiliate networks. For example, if you're in the tech niche, you might explore networks like Impact Radius or AvantLink.

Check E-commerce Platforms:
- If your niche involves physical products, consider looking at popular e-commerce platforms. Amazon Associates is one of

the largest and most versatile affiliate programs, covering a wide range of products.

Visit Company Websites:

- Visit the websites of companies or brands within your niche. Look for "Affiliate Program," "Partners," or "Become an Affiliate" in the website's footer or menu.

Utilize Social Media:

- Search for affiliate programs on social media platforms. Companies often promote their affiliate programs on platforms like Twitter, LinkedIn, or Instagram.

Read Reviews and Recommendations:

- Look for reviews and recommendations from other affiliates in your niche. Online forums, blogs, and social media groups can be valuable resources for learning about the experiences of others.

Evaluate Commission Rates and Terms:

- Compare commission rates, payment terms, and cookie durations (the time between a user clicking your affiliate link and making a purchase) for different programs. Choose programs that offer competitive rates and fair terms.

Apply and Get Approved:

- Once you've identified potential affiliate programs, follow the application process on their website. Some programs may have specific requirements or may need to review your content before approving your application.

Remember to comply with the terms and conditions of each affiliate program, and disclose your affiliate relationships transparently to your audience. Building trust with your audience is crucial for a successful affiliate marketing strategy.

Implementing effective strategies to promote affiliate products and earn commissions

Promoting affiliate products effectively requires a combination of strategic planning, understanding your target audience, and utilizing various marketing channels. Here's a step-by-step guide to help you implement effective strategies:

1. Choose the Right Affiliate Products:

- Select products that align with your niche and are relevant to your audience.
- Consider products with high commissions and a good reputation.

2. Understand Your Audience:

- Create buyer personas to understand your audience's needs, preferences, and pain points.
- Tailor your promotions to address your audience's specific concerns.

3. Build a Trustworthy Platform:

- Establish a professional-looking website or blog.
- Provide valuable content regularly to build trust with your audience.
- Disclose your affiliate relationships transparently.

4. Utilize Content Marketing:

- Create high-quality, informative content related to the affiliate products.
- Use blog posts, articles, videos, and other formats to educate and engage your audience.
- Incorporate SEO best practices to enhance discoverability.

5. Leverage Email Marketing:

- Build an email list to nurture leads.
- Send targeted emails with product recommendations, reviews, and exclusive deals.
- Use segmentation to tailor your messages to different audience segments.

6. Social Media Promotion:

- Identify the social media platforms where your audience is most active.
- Share engaging content, including product reviews, testimonials, and promotions.
- Utilize paid advertising on social media platforms if it fits your budget.

7. Create Compelling Reviews and Tutorials:

- Write in-depth product reviews highlighting benefits and features.
- Develop tutorials showing how the product solves a problem or improves users' lives.

8. Utilize Visual Content:

- Use eye-catching visuals, such as infographics and images, to enhance your content.
- Create engaging videos that demonstrate the product's use and advantages.

9. Run Contests and Giveaways:

- Encourage user participation through contests and giveaways.
- Require participants to share your affiliate link or follow specific social media accounts for entry.

10. Stay Updated and Adapt:

- Keep abreast of industry trends and product updates.
- Adapt your strategies based on performance analytics and feedback.

11. Optimize for Conversions:

- Use persuasive call-to-action (CTA) buttons.
- Experiment with different placement and wording of your affiliate links.

12. Track and Analyze Performance:

- Use analytics tools to track the performance of your affiliate links.
- Identify what works and refine your strategies accordingly.

13. Build Relationships with Merchants:

- Communicate with affiliate managers to get insider information, promotional materials, and exclusive deals.
- Network with other affiliates to share insights and strategies.

14. Compliance and Disclosure:

- Adhere to legal and ethical guidelines for affiliate marketing.
- Clearly disclose your affiliate relationships to maintain trust with your audience.

Remember, success in affiliate marketing takes time, consistency, and ongoing refinement of your strategies based on performance data and industry changes.

Chapter 6: Blogging and Content Monetization

Creating a successful blog or website with valuable and interesting content

Creating a successful blog or website with valuable and interesting content involves a combination of thoughtful planning, consistent effort, and attention to your audience's needs. Here are some steps to guide you through the process:

1. Define Your Niche:

- Choose a specific and well-defined niche that aligns with your interests and expertise.
- Consider your target audience and what kind of content they are likely to find valuable.

2. Know Your Audience:

- Understand your target audience's preferences, interests, and problems.
- Create content that addresses their needs and provides solutions.

3. Set Clear Goals:

- Define your goals for the blog or website. These could include increasing traffic, building an email list, or monetizing through ads or products.

4. Create a Content Strategy:

- Plan your content in advance, including topics, formats (e.g., articles, videos, infographics), and posting schedule.
- Mix up your content to keep it interesting and engaging.

5. Invest in Quality Content:

- Create well-researched, informative, and original content.
- Use visuals like images, videos, and infographics to enhance your content.

6. Optimize for SEO:

- Conduct keyword research and optimize your content for search engines.
- Use descriptive and compelling titles, meta descriptions, and headers.

7. Build a Strong Brand:

- Create a memorable and cohesive brand for your blog or website.
- Consistent branding helps in building trust and recognition.

8. Engage with Your Audience:

- Respond to comments and engage with your audience on social media.
- Consider creating a community around your blog, such as a forum or Facebook group.

9. Utilize Social Media:

- Share your content on relevant social media platforms.
- Tailor your approach to each platform and use a mix of media types.

10. Optimize for Mobile:

- Ensure your website is mobile-friendly as a significant portion of internet users access content on mobile devices.

11. Monetization Strategies:

- Explore various monetization options such as ads, affiliate marketing, sponsored content, or selling products/services.
- Diversify your income streams to reduce reliance on a single source.

12. Analytics and Improvement:

- Use analytics tools to track the performance of your content.
- Analyze what works and what doesn't, and make adjustments accordingly.

13. Email Marketing:

- Build an email list and use email marketing to connect with your audience.
- Provide value in your emails and avoid being overly promotional.

14. Stay Consistent:

- Consistency is key. Stick to your content schedule and stay committed to your goals.

15. Learn and Adapt:

- Stay updated on industry trends and adapt your strategy accordingly.
- Continuously improve based on feedback and data.

Remember, building a successful blog or website takes time and persistence. Stay patient, stay true to your niche, and consistently deliver value to your audience.

Monetizing your blog through advertising, sponsored posts, and affiliate marketing

Monetizing your blog through advertising, sponsored posts, and affiliate marketing can be a lucrative way to generate income. Here's a breakdown of each method:

Advertising:
- **Display Ads: You can join ad networks like Google AdSense, Media.net, or AdThrive to display ads on your blog. These networks pay you based on clicks or impressions.**
- **Direct Ad Sales: Once your blog gains traction, you can directly sell ad space to businesses relevant to your niche. This can be more lucrative than ad networks.**

Sponsored Posts:
- **Companies may pay you to write posts about their products or services. Make sure sponsored content aligns with your blog's niche and interests your audience.**
- **Clearly disclose sponsored posts to maintain transparency and trust with your readers.**

Affiliate Marketing:
- **Promote products or services and earn a commission for each sale or lead generated through your unique affiliate link.**
- **Choose affiliate products relevant to your niche to ensure they resonate with your audience.**
- **Disclose affiliate relationships to maintain transparency.**

Email Marketing:
- **Build an email list and use it to promote affiliate products, sponsored content, or your products/services directly.**
- **Provide value to your subscribers through newsletters, exclusive content, or special offers.**

Create and Sell Products:
- **Develop and sell your products, such as eBooks, online courses, merchandise, or any other items relevant to your niche.**

- Utilize your blog and social media platforms to market and sell these products.

Membership and Subscription Models:
- Offer premium content or a membership area on your blog for a subscription fee.
- Patreon or similar platforms can be used to offer exclusive content to paying subscribers.

Webinars and Online Events:
- Host webinars, workshops, or online events and charge participants.
- This can be a great way to share knowledge and engage with your audience while generating income.

Freelancing and Consulting:
- Showcase your expertise through your blog and offer freelance or consulting services.
- Advertise your services on your blog, and leverage your reputation and expertise to attract clients.

Remember to focus on providing value to your audience. Quality content and authenticity are crucial for building and maintaining trust. Additionally, diversify your income streams to reduce dependence on a single source. Regularly assess the performance of each monetization method and adjust your strategy accordingly.

Building and engaging an audience to increase your blog's earning potential

Building and engaging an audience is crucial for increasing your blog's earning potential. Here are some effective strategies to help you achieve this:

Define Your Niche:
- Clearly define your blog's niche to attract a specific audience interested in your content.
- Specializing in a niche helps you stand out and target a more engaged audience.

Create High-Quality Content:
- Produce valuable, well-researched, and engaging content.
- Solve problems, answer questions, and provide unique insights to keep your audience coming back.

Consistent Posting Schedule:
- Establish a consistent posting schedule to keep your audience engaged and aware of when to expect new content.
- Consistency helps build trust and loyalty.

Social Media Promotion:
- Share your blog posts on social media platforms to reach a wider audience.
- Utilize platforms like Facebook, Twitter, Instagram, LinkedIn, and Pinterest based on your audience's preferences.

Engage with Your Audience:
- Respond to comments on your blog and social media.
- Ask questions and encourage discussions.
- Conduct polls and surveys to involve your audience in decision-making.

Email Marketing:
- Build an email list to directly reach your audience.
- Send regular newsletters with updates, exclusive content, and offers to keep your audience engaged.

Collaborate with Others:
- Collaborate with other bloggers, influencers, or industry experts.
- Guest post on other blogs or invite guest bloggers to contribute to your site.

Optimize for SEO:
- Optimize your blog for search engines to increase organic traffic.

- Use relevant keywords, meta tags, and create SEO-friendly content.

Offer Freebies and Incentives:
- Provide free downloadable resources, such as eBooks, templates, or guides.
- Host giveaways or contests to encourage participation.

Monetize Strategically:
- Use a mix of monetization methods, such as affiliate marketing, sponsored posts, advertising, and selling digital products.
- Ensure that your monetization strategies align with your audience's interests and needs.

Analytics and Feedback:
- Use analytics tools to track the performance of your content and audience engagement.
- Pay attention to feedback and adjust your strategy accordingly.

Build a Community:
- Create a sense of community by fostering connections among your audience members.
- Consider creating forums, discussion groups, or social media groups related to your niche.

Remember, building and engaging an audience takes time and patience.

Consistently delivering value and actively participating in your community

will contribute to long-term success.

Chapter 7: Online Trading and Investments

Exploring the world of online trading, including stocks, forex, and cryptocurrencies

Exploring the world of online trading can be both exciting and challenging. Each type of trading, whether it's stocks, forex (foreign

exchange), or cryptocurrencies, has its own set of characteristics, risks, and strategies. Here's a brief overview of each:

Stock Trading:
- **What it is:** Buying and selling shares of publicly traded companies on stock exchanges.
- **How it works:** Investors can buy shares of a company and potentially profit from the company's success through dividends or capital gains.
- **Risks:** Stock prices can be influenced by various factors, including economic conditions, company performance, and market sentiment.
- **Tips:** Research companies thoroughly, diversify your portfolio, and keep an eye on market trends.

Forex Trading:
- **What it is:** Forex (foreign exchange) trading involves buying and selling currencies in the global marketplace.
- **How it works:** Traders speculate on the relative value of one currency against another, aiming to profit from currency price movements.
- **Risks:** Currency markets can be volatile, influenced by geopolitical events, economic data, and central bank policies.
- **Tips:** Understand the factors that influence currency movements, use risk management strategies, and stay informed about global economic events.

Cryptocurrency Trading:
- **What it is:** buying and selling digital currencies like Bitcoin, Ethereum, and other altcoins.
- **How it works:** Cryptocurrencies operate on decentralized blockchain technology. Traders aim to profit from price fluctuations.
- **Risks:** Cryptocurrency markets are known for their volatility. Regulatory developments, security concerns, and market sentiment can impact prices.

- **Tips:** Stay informed about the technology, use secure wallets, and be cautious about the high volatility in the crypto market.

General Tips for Online Trading:

Education: Before starting, educate yourself on the basics of the market you're interested in. Understand the terminology, market dynamics, and risk factors.
Risk Management: Set clear risk management strategies, including stop-loss orders to limit potential losses.
Diversification: Spread your investments across different assets to reduce risk.
Stay Informed: Keep abreast of market news, economic indicators, and any developments that may impact your chosen market.
Demo Trading: Consider using demo accounts provided by many platforms to practice trading without risking real money.
Choose a Reputable Platform: Select a reliable and secure trading platform. Check for regulatory compliance and user reviews.
Start Small: Begin with a small amount of capital that you can afford to lose while you gain experience.

Remember, online trading involves risks, and it's important to approach it with caution. If you're new to trading, consider seeking advice from financial professionals and gradually increase your involvement as you become more comfortable and experienced.

Learning the basics of investing and managing a diversified portfolio

Certainly! Learning the basics of investing and managing a diversified portfolio is an important step towards building long-term wealth. Here's a guide to help you get started:

1. Understand Your Financial Goals:

- Determine your financial objectives, such as saving for retirement, buying a home, or funding your children's education. Your goals will shape your investment strategy.

2. Educate Yourself:

- Learn the basics of investment types, such as stocks, bonds, and mutual funds. Understand the associated risks and potential returns.

3. Risk Tolerance:

- Assess your risk tolerance. This is influenced by your age, financial situation, and comfort level with market fluctuations. Generally, younger investors can take on more risk.

4. Create a Budget:

- Establish a budget to ensure you have sufficient funds for both investing and your daily expenses.

5. Emergency Fund:

- Before investing, build an emergency fund equivalent to 3-6 months of living expenses. This provides a financial cushion in case of unexpected expenses.

6. Diversification:

- Spread your investments across different asset classes (stocks, bonds, real estate) to reduce risk. Diversification helps minimize the impact of poor-performing investments on your overall portfolio.

7. Asset Allocation:

- Determine the right mix of assets based on your risk tolerance and investment goals. This is known as asset allocation. Rebalance your portfolio periodically to maintain your desired asset allocation.

8. Investment Accounts:

- Consider tax-advantaged accounts like IRAs and 401(k)s for retirement savings. These accounts offer tax benefits that can enhance your returns over time.

9. Stocks:

- Understand how stocks work, including market orders, limit orders, and the factors that influence stock prices. Consider investing in a diverse range of industries to reduce risk.

10. Bonds:

- Learn about bonds and how they provide income through interest payments. Understand the relationship between bond prices and interest rates.

11. Mutual Funds and ETFs:

- Explore mutual funds and exchange-traded funds (ETFs) for instant diversification. These funds pool money from multiple investors to invest in a diversified portfolio of stocks or bonds.

12. Stay Informed:

- Regularly update your knowledge about the financial markets, economic trends, and any changes in your investments.

13. Long-Term Perspective:

- Investing is a long-term endeavor. Avoid making impulsive decisions based on short-term market fluctuations.

14. Professional Advice:

- **Consider consulting with a financial advisor, especially if you're new to investing or have a complex financial situation.**

15. Review and Adjust:

- **Periodically review your portfolio to ensure it aligns with your goals. Adjust your investments as your financial situation and goals evolve.**

Remember, everyone's financial situation is unique, so it's essential to tailor your investment strategy to your specific needs and risk tolerance. Additionally, be patient and disciplined, as successful investing takes time and a well-thought-out approach.

Mitigating risks and maximizing profits in online trading and investing

Mitigating risks and maximizing profits in online trading and investing require a combination of strategic planning, risk management, and staying informed about market trends. Here are some key principles to consider:

Risk Mitigation Strategies:

Diversification:
- Spread your investments across different asset classes (stocks, bonds, commodities) to reduce the impact of a poor-performing investment on your overall portfolio.

Risk Tolerance Assessment:
- Understand your risk tolerance and invest accordingly. Don't invest more than you can afford to lose.

Stop-Loss Orders:
- Set stop-loss orders to limit potential losses. These orders automatically sell a security when it reaches a predetermined price, helping you minimize losses.

Research and Due Diligence:
- Thoroughly research and understand the assets you're investing in. Stay informed about market trends, company news, and economic indicators.

Stay Updated on Market News:
- Follow financial news regularly to be aware of any factors that might impact your investments.

Use Technical and Fundamental Analysis:
- Combine both technical and fundamental analysis to make more informed investment decisions. Technical analysis involves studying price charts, while fundamental analysis involves evaluating a company's financial health.

Risk-Adjusted Returns:
- Evaluate investments not just on potential returns but also on the risk involved. Consider the risk-adjusted returns to make more balanced decisions.

Profit Maximization Strategies:

Have a Clear Investment Plan:
- Define your financial goals and create a clear investment plan. This will help you make decisions based on a strategy rather than emotions.

Regularly Review and Rebalance Portfolio:
- Periodically review your portfolio to ensure it aligns with your goals and risk tolerance. Rebalance as necessary to maintain your desired asset allocation.

Utilize Dollar-Cost Averaging:
- Invest a fixed amount at regular intervals, regardless of market conditions. This strategy can help average out the impact of market volatility.

Long-Term Perspective:
- Adopt a long-term perspective rather than attempting to time the market. Long-term investing often outperforms short-term speculation.

Stay Disciplined:
- Stick to your investment plan and avoid making impulsive decisions based on short-term market fluctuations.

Continuous Learning:
- Stay informed about new investment opportunities, market trends, and changes in economic conditions. Continuous learning can help you adapt to evolving market dynamics.

Use Limit Orders:
- When buying or selling securities, consider using limit orders to specify the price at which you are willing to execute a trade. This can help you avoid unexpected price fluctuations.

Remember, there is no foolproof strategy, and all investments carry some level of risk. It's crucial to tailor your approach to your individual financial situation, risk tolerance, and investment goals. Consulting with a financial advisor can also provide personalized guidance based on your specific circumstances.

Anticipating and preparing for the future of making money online

Anticipating and preparing for the future of making money online requires staying informed about emerging trends, understanding market dynamics, and adapting to technological advancements. Here are some strategies and considerations to help you navigate the evolving landscape of online income generation:

Stay Informed:
- **Follow Industry Trends: Keep an eye on trends in digital marketing, e-commerce, and technology. Subscribe to industry blogs, attend webinars, and participate in relevant online communities to stay updated.**
- **Tech News: Stay informed about technological advancements, as they can impact online business models. Technologies like blockchain, artificial**

intelligence, and augmented reality are continually evolving and may present new opportunities.

Diversify Income Streams:

- Multiple Platforms: Diversify your presence across various online platforms to reduce dependence on a single source of income. This could include e-commerce platforms, freelance websites, social media, and more.
- Passive Income: Explore opportunities for passive income streams, such as affiliate marketing, selling digital products, or investing. Passive income allows you to earn money with less ongoing effort.

Skill Development:

- Adaptability: Develop a growth mindset and be open to acquiring new skills. The online landscape is dynamic, and being adaptable is crucial for long-term success.
- Learn Emerging Technologies: Stay updated on emerging technologies relevant to your field. For example, if you're in content creation, learn about virtual reality or augmented reality content creation.

Build a Strong Online Presence:

- Personal Branding: Invest in building a strong personal brand. This can enhance your credibility and attract more opportunities.
- Quality Content: Create high-quality and valuable content. This not only helps in building a loyal audience but also enhances your visibility in search engines and on social media.

E-commerce and Online Marketplaces:

- Explore New Platforms: Keep an eye on emerging e-commerce platforms and online marketplaces. Consider expanding your product offerings or services to reach a broader audience.
- Dropshipping and Print on Demand: Explore dropshipping or print-on-demand business models, which allow you to sell products without holding inventory.

Remote Work and Freelancing:
- **Freelancing Opportunities:** If applicable to your skills, consider freelancing or remote work opportunities. Platforms like Upwork, Fiverr, and others provide a global marketplace for various skills.

Cybersecurity and Privacy:
- **Security Measures:** As online transactions increase, prioritize cybersecurity and ensure that your online activities are secure. This is crucial for building trust with your audience and protecting your financial assets.

Legal and Regulatory Compliance:
- **Stay Compliant:** Understand and comply with relevant legal and regulatory frameworks in your industry. This is especially important as online business activities are subject to various laws.

Remember that the online landscape is constantly evolving, so regularly reassess your strategies and be ready to adapt to new opportunities and challenges. Keep networking, learning, and refining your approach to stay ahead in the dynamic world of making money online.

Conclusion: The Journey to Financial Freedom

Reflecting on your progress and achievements in making money online provides valuable insights into the journey you've undertaken. Take a moment to celebrate the milestones you've reached, acknowledging the dedication and effort invested in your online ventures. Whether it's reaching a certain income level, building a solid online presence, or mastering new skills, recognize and appreciate your accomplishments.

As you reflect, consider the lessons learned from challenges and setbacks. They are stepping stones to growth and improvement. Use these experiences to refine your strategies, optimize your approaches, and enhance your resilience in the dynamic landscape of online entrepreneurship.

Setting new goals and aspirations is essential for sustaining momentum and driving continuous progress. Define clear, realistic, and measurable objectives that align with your overarching vision. Whether it's expanding your online presence, diversifying income streams, or mastering emerging trends, set targets that inspire and challenge you.

Embrace the potential for financial freedom and success through online entrepreneurship. Recognize the limitless opportunities that

the digital realm offers. The ability to reach a global audience, leverage automation tools, and adapt to evolving market trends positions you for unprecedented growth. Cultivate a mindset that sees challenges as opportunities and failures as valuable lessons on the path to success.

Stay agile and open to innovation, embracing the dynamic nature of online business. Leverage your strengths, continually learn, and adapt to emerging technologies and market shifts. Financial freedom awaits those who are proactive, persistent, and willing to evolve with the ever-changing landscape of online entrepreneurship.

In summary, reflecting on your journey, setting ambitious yet achievable goals, and embracing the potential for financial freedom through online entrepreneurship are integral steps in your continued success. Celebrate your achievements, learn from challenges, and approach the future with optimism, determination, and a strategic mindset.

Regenerate